10 Tales Jesus Told

10 Tales Jesus Told

Story Rhyme for Young and Old

RUTH BUCKLEY

THANKFUL BOOKS

First published in 2010 by
Thankful Books, P.O. Box 2118, Seaford, BN25 9AR, UK

ISBN: 978 1 905084 22 7

Bible quotations are from the Holy Bible,
New International Version © 1973, 1978, 1984 by
the International Bible Society

Book design and production for the publisher by
Bookprint Creative Services, <www.bookprint.co.uk>
Printed in Great Britain.

For everyone
who loves the stories of Jesus

God bless you

Contents

1. The Sower and the Seed   9

2. The Kingdom of Heaven Is like Treasure   17

3. Saved by a Samaritan   21

4. The Kingdom of Heaven Is like a Crop of Wheat   35

5. A Son Who Just Wanted Fun   39

6. The Kingdom of Heaven Is like Yeast   53

7. The Builder Who Bungled   57

8. The Kingdom of Heaven Is like a Seed   71

9. The Bridesmaids Who Blew it   77

10. The Kingdom of Heaven Is like a Net   89

oOo

1.

The Sower and the Seed

On one occasion Jesus began to teach by the lake.
The crowd that gathered around him was so large that he
got into a boat and sat in it out on the lake. . . .
He taught them many things by parables and in his teaching
said, 'Listen! A farmer went out to sow some seeds . . .'
Mark 4:1–20

When Jesus came he had cool tales to tell,
stories of God and of heaven or hell.
He told of the things that he
        saw every day,
and used them to teach his disciples God's way.

One hot, sunny day while Jesus was walking
along with his friends and quietly talking,
he went by a field that was
                ploughed up all round,
and saw how a farmer sowed seeds on the ground.
They stopped and they watched
                as he walked to and fro,
hoping his seeds would take root and grow.

But when Jesus stopped the crowds gathered near:
he had stories to tell and they wanted to hear.

So he took the big crowd to a wide, sandy beach
on the Galilee lake, and just within reach
was a fisherman's boat,
                moored ready to sail,
and Jesus sat there while he told them this tale.

A farmer was wanting to grow some wheat
to make into bread
           for his children to eat.
So he went to his barn and got out his plough,
he went to his pasture
        and brought in his cow.
He yoked up his cow and his plough both together,
and choosing a day that had
           warm, sunny weather,
he ploughed up the field from bottom to top
to make it all ready for sowing the crop.

*B*ut some of the stony ground needed hard toil,
and some ground had thistles
             and thorns in the soil,
and blackbirds and seagulls were flying around
to pick up the insects
        and worms in the ground,
but the farmer kept working all through the long day,
and only went home with the
           very last sun-ray.

*T*he next day he got up bright and early,
and went outside while the sky was pearly.
He went to his barn and
         took down his bag,
and filled it with seeds till his shoulder sagged.

Then he went to his field and walked all around
throwing handfuls of seeds
                out onto the ground.

But some of the seeds went onto the pathway,
and birds came and gobbled it up,
                where it lay;
and some seeds fell onto the hard, stony soil,
where the sun dried it up and made the seeds spoil;
and some seeds fell into
          the thorns and the weeds,
which quickly grew up and choked all the seeds.

But some of the seeds,
                    as he walked up and down,
fell into soil that was crumbly and brown,
and safe where the plough
                had made a deep furrow,
they quickly took root and started to grow.

Then, on the good soil,
                  the wheat in the field
grew thirty or sixty times more: what a yield!
But at harvest time some of the
                good soil had grown
a crop of one hundred times more than he'd sown!

So the farmer was able to harvest the wheat,
to make into bread
            for his children to eat.

When all of the people had gone home to bed,
and Jesus had finished,
          his friends came and said,
'You've told us this tale about things that we've seen,
but what do the soil and the seeds really mean?'
So Jesus sat down
       and began to unfold
the meaning behind this cool tale he had told.

'The seed is the word of God, sent from above.
The soil is the hearts of the people God loves.

'The birds are like Satan who enters their thoughts,
and snatches away the words I have taught.
For Satan can whisper
           those negative things
that make them reject the message I bring.

'The weeds are the busy things choking their mind:

they don't think of God as they never have time!
They want to acquire things,
                              they want better pay;
in the struggles of life my words slip away.

'The stones stop my words
                              going deep in their hearts:
the seeds will dry up because roots cannot start.
They are joyful at first to take in my words,
but when trouble comes
         they forget what they've heard.

'But the good soil are hearts that drink in my words;
they want to know more,
                              and love what they've heard.
A harvest of good things, like love, joy and peace
will grow in their hearts
                              from out of the seeds.'

This story of Jesus can help us to know
that our hearts are like soil
         where God's word can grow.
Not everyone's heart is quite ready for God:
some find his words hard and they
                              can't feel his love.

But God's love is strong,

it can change people's hearts,
to become like the good soil, so new life can start.

2.

The Kingdom of Heaven Is like Treasure

Jesus said, 'The kingdom of heaven is like treasure
hidden in a field.
When a man found it, he hid it again,
and then in his joy went and sold all that he had
and bought that field.'
Matthew 13:44

The kingdom of heaven
is like treasure
that's hidden away
in the ground,
but think how the smallest
measure of treasure
is a magnet
for people around!

Just pick up a whiff
of some treasure;
the feeling is really unique.
There's a buzz of excitement,
a tingle of pleasure,
when you think
there is treasure
to seek!

Just think, if you're digging
for treasure
and you find a brooch
or some gold,
that was worn long ago
by a lady of leisure
and valued by people of old.

What if you could purchase
that treasure?
Wouldn't you sell
all your things,
for the value and pleasure
of beautiful treasure
like gold or diamonds
or rings?

The kingdom of heaven
is like treasure,
treasure that's hidden away.
A true faith in God is valued
like treasure,
and people find it
each day.

And when they've discovered
this treasure,
some might give up
all they own.
For the worth of the treasure
can never be measured.
In the whole of their lives
they feel no greater pleasure
than to live
for that treasure alone.

3.
Saved
by a Samaritan

On one occasion an expert in the law stood up
to test Jesus. 'Teacher,' he asked, 'what must I do
to inherit eternal life?' . . .
Luke 10:25–37

When Jesus was discussing his teaching one day
with a group of Rabbis
            of the Jewish faith,
a lawyer who studied the laws of the Jews
stood up to question
        and test Jesus' views.
'So what should I do then, good teacher,' he said,
'to inherit eternal life
                when I'm dead?'
'Now, you are a lawyer and you are a Jew,' Jesus said,
'what does the law command you to do?'

The lawyer had read all the laws God had given,
and learnt to recite them
        as they had been written.
He knew the right answer straight out of his head.
'You must love the Lord your God,'
                    he said,
'with all of your soul and with all of your heart,
with all of your mind and with
            all of your strength.'
Then he added some more, 'The law says as well,
you must love your neighbour as much as yourself.'

'That's right,' Jesus said, 'do all of these things,
and you will have life that is everlasting!'

_B_ut the lawyer frowned and looked disappointed.
It wasn't the answer
      he felt that he wanted.
He thought he was good and obeyed all God's law;
he didn't need Jesus to tell him,
                'Do more!'
'So who is my neighbour?' he asked, feeling cross
and hoping to catch Jesus
          out at a loss.
So Jesus then told them a cool tale indeed
how someone showed love to a neighbour in need.

'_T_here once was a time,' Jesus said to those men,
'when a businessman lived
            in Jerusalem.
He decided one morning, a long time ago
that he needed to travel to Jericho.'

_N_ow in those old days, when they travelled away,
it wasn't like journeys that
            we make today.
They didn't have bicycles, cars or trains.
They didn't have scooters,
          buses or planes.
No, all that they had was their feet,
      in the past,
a horse, or a donkey, they never went fast.

They didn't have good, tarmac roads
                    for their trips,
just rough, rocky pathways with slippery dips.
They didn't have grass with
                big trees and green leaves,
just wild, lonely country, with bandits and thieves.

The businessman needed this journey a lot,
so his well-laden donkey
                    set off with a trot.
He knew that the way would be wild and rough;
he travelled alone, it was going to be tough,
so he left from Jerusalem
                in the first light,
to get down to Jericho by that same night.

At first it went well, he was in a good mood,
the roadway was wide
            and the going was smooth.
His donkey was fresh and was making good time,
and he thought that the journey was going to be fine.
He met a few friends and he
                    talked of the day,
but found they were going a different way.

But then, as he travelled away from the town,

the road became hilly,
                        it went up and down;
the country got wilder, he saw flocks of sheep;
the hillside got nearer,
                        the path became steep;
the donkey got slower and tired with each tread;
there was no-one behind them
        and no-one ahead.
He got a bit worried and looked all around,
but no-one was there, not even a sound.

Then a horrible shout
                made him stop with a shock,
as a big gang of robbers jumped out from a rock.

It seemed like an army had come to attack,
as knocking him down from the
                        donkey's broad back,
they kicked him and punched at his head where he lay,
while somebody led the old donkey away!

Then, quite suddenly, the onslaught was over;
the thieves and the bandits
                ran into the cover.
They left the man bleeding from bruises and cuts,
as he lay on the path in the dust and the ruts.

The rascals had stolen
　　　　everything that he owned,
and left him a victim, abandoned, alone!

The man was half dead and could only just groan,
would somebody help him,
　　　　　　　and get him back home?
Perhaps someone kind from Jerusalem city,
would see he was bleeding, and show him some pity?

A long time went by before someone came past,
then a priest from Jerusalem
　　　　　　　came up at last.
Perhaps he was thinking big thoughts of his own,
and missed the hurt man, till his horse heard a groan.
When the horse started rearing
　　　　and prancing around,
he saw the man lying, quite still, on the ground.

The priest gave a start, -
　　　　　　feeling shocked at the sight,
and pulled up his big horse as if to alight.
But he sat and he stared at the man, feeling stunned,
and wondered whether
　　　　　　to stay or to run.

'Perhaps he is dead, and I know it seems mean,
but touching dead bodies
will make me unclean.
I would have to stop working and doing my job,
and besides all that, I don't want to get robbed!'

So he hastily spurred his big horse to a trot,
and left the poor man in that terrible spot!

Not long after that
the next person who passed,
was a man called a Levite, he walked very fast.
He was toiling along the steep path
on his own,
when he suddenly noticed a very weak moan.
He looked all around,
and his heart almost jumped,
at the terrible wounds of the man, lying slumped.

He took it all in with a quick, startled glance,
then backed right away from him,
keeping his distance.
Then he fearfully looked at the menacing hills,
in case any bandits were hiding there still.
Then with one last look,
he ran off round the bend,

anxious to get to his long journey's end.

'I can't help that man as I'm all on my own,
and I've got nothing with me to carry him home!
I mustn't stay now,
                it's getting quite late.'
and he left the poor man to his horrible fate! . . .

A Samaritan man was the next to arrive,
and by now the hurt man
                must be hardly alive.
The donkey was plodding along with its load
when it sensed there was something ahead on the road.
It suddenly stopped
        and refused to go on,
and when the man nudged it, it brayed loud and long.

The Samaritan got off and walked on ahead,
and almost fell over the man,
                who seemed dead.
He got on his knees on the ground by the man
thinking, 'What a bad thing!
        I must do what I can.'
He saw, from his clothes, that the man was a Jew,
and the good Samaritan already knew
that the Jews and Samaritans
                did not get along,

but that did not make him decide to get gone!

The Jews then despised the Samaritan race
but there on the road,
                              in that terrible place,
the Samaritan knew that the Jew needed help,
and would probably die there if left by himself!

The poor Jew, by then, was barely alive,
but the good Samaritan
                         helped him survive!
He searched through his luggage and opened his bags;
he got out some wine, some oil and clean rags.
He poured on the wine
          to clean up his wounds,
and added the oil to help them heal soon.
Then he bandaged the wounded man
                              all nice and neat,
from the top of his head to the soles of his feet.

Then the good Samaritan
                         picked up the Jew,
taking care that he did not hurt him anew,
and put him right over
                    the old donkey's back,
and walked with the donkey along the rough track.

He soon found an inn for his unconscious guest,
and paid for a room
        where the poor man could rest.
Then he asked them to make up a clean, comfy bed,
and saw that the man would be warm
            and well fed.

Next day the Samaritan wanted to leave,
so to make very sure
            that the man would receive
the very best care, he got out his purse,
and said to the innkeeper,
        'Please get him a nurse!
Here's two silver coins, and when I come back,
I will pay you for anything else
            that you lack.'
Then he said to himself, 'I've done all that I can!'
and went on his journey a happier man.

Then Jesus turned back to the lawyer and asked,
'One of the travellers that day who passed,
showed neighbourly love
            to the poor wounded man.
Was it the priest, the Levite or the Samaritan?'
'I know,' said the lawyer,
                looking sad and grim,
'only the Samaritan showed love to him!'

'You're right,' said Jesus,
                    'if you love God's name
and follow his laws, you must do the same!'

This story of Jesus shows how much it's worth
for people to live for God here on the earth.
The Samaritan man
          was despised by the race
of the poor wounded man, yet he had the grace
to forget any difference,
                    ignore every danger,
and give up his journey to save the poor stranger.

Now Jesus is called the Good Samaritan,
for his life was unselfish,
                    just like this man.
He cared for hurt people, whatever it cost,
till he give up his life to save those who are lost.
And even today
          his love is still there
to rescue the people in need of his care.

But Jesus needs followers
          to help in his work
and show out his love to the people on earth.

So people who love God,
                    who God makes brand-new,
must always be ready to love others too.

oOo

4.

The Kingdom of Heaven
Is like a
Crop of Wheat

Jesus said to them, 'This is what the kingdom of God is like.
A man scatters seed on the ground.
Night or day, whether he sleeps or gets up, the seed
sprouts and grows,
though he does not know how . . . .'
Mark 4:26–29

The kingdom of heaven is like
a crop of wheat
which a farmer sows as seeds
in his field.
He hopes the seeds will grow and,
when harvest is complete,
his field will yield
a good amount of wheat.

But after he has sown the seeds
the farmer goes away,
and carries on with all his work around.
He goes to bed at night,
he gets up in the day,
and leaves the wheat seeds lying
in the ground.

Yet if he sat and watched them
and worried if they'd grow,
he couldn't make the wheat grow
any more.
He knows that, of their own accord,
the shoots will start to show,
and the field will yield its harvest
as before.

It's a mystery to the farmer when the
first blade will appear,
or why the stalks of wheat
grow tall and thin,
or how the sun and rain
make grain
swell in the ear.
He only knows that when it's ripe,
the harvest can begin.

The kingdom of heaven is like
the crop of wheat;
the word of God is like
the farmer's seed.
The word grows slowly in our souls,
it's silent and discrete,
but in good time
God makes the crop succeed.

And when the crop is ripe and the
end of time has come,
then God will reap the harvest
he has sown,
and the souls of those who love him,
the crop that he has won,
will be with him
inside his heavenly home.

5.

A Son Who
Just Wanted Fun

Jesus said: 'There was a man who had two sons. The younger son said to his father, "Father give me my share of the estate." So he divided his property between them. . . .'
Luke 15:11–32

Jesus loved everyone, wealthy or poor;
he welcomed the people
                    who came to his door;
the good people, bad people, sick ones or well;
the ones with good lives
          or the ones who rebelled.
He taught them of God and he made them his friends,
and told them good stories again and again.
He cured their sick bodies,
                    he healed broken hearts,
he helped them be different and make a new start.

But Jesus found 'good' people disliked the 'bad'
not knowing that he understood
          and was sad.
'He'll get a bad name if he mixes with them!'
They started to gossip, complain and condemn,
but then Jesus told them
                    a tale of a son
whose life went all wrong when he just wanted fun.

There once was a farmer, a big, wealthy man;
he owned a good farmyard,
                    a house and some land.
His beautiful wife and his two healthy sons

were waiting at home when his day's work was done.

With his arm round his wife and his boys on his knees,
there wasn't a man
        more contented and pleased.
'I've worked all these years and I've built a good farm,'
he said to his wife, as she sat in his arm,
'and when I grow old
            these sons will inherit
my house and my farmyard and all that is in it.'

The years went by quickly, the boys grew to men,
but turned out to be very different by then.
The older son grew to be
            steady and calm,
and started to work for his dad on the farm.

But the younger son grew to be spoilt and reckless.
He got into trouble,
        was carefree and feckless.
He went to wild parties with friends who were bad:
the last thing he wanted
            was to work for his dad!
His father got worried, his mum told him off,
but all that he did was to scorn them and scoff.

*B*ut . . . the older son calmly kept working along,
and silently watched
                     as his brother went wrong.

*T*he younger son soon became
                          fed up at home.
He wanted to travel, to wander and roam.
'I wish I could get right away and be me.
I just want to see things,
                    enjoy life, be free!' . . .

*Y*et to fund this adventure he needed some cash,
so he went to his father
                       and quite simply asked,
'Hey Dad, you remember the money you said
is going to be mine on the
         day you are dead?
I want it right now, to start up on my own:
a young man can't always be
                  staying at home!'

*T*he farmer was troubled, he loved his young son,
and often gave in when he
                   wanted some fun.
'But this time it means I must sell up some land,
I'll talk to your mum as it's not on my plan.'

The farmer went off
                and he talked to his wife,
'If we refuse this, he will just give us strife!'

So he called in his agent and sold up some land,
and gave all the cash to his son,
                    in his hand.

Both parents were sad when they saw him depart;
they had a few worries deep down
        in their heart.
'Let's hope he is wise and he uses it well;
he might do some good, only time will tell!'
But . . . the older brother
              just worked on alone,
and silently watched as the young man left home.

The son set out gladly with no backward glances,
off into the big world
               to try out his chances,
but the cash in his pocket was burning a hole,
as he sauntered along with
        a casual stroll.
So he stopped in a café and made some cool friends,
and soon he was drinking and
           starting to spend.

*H*e went to some parties and had a fab time;
he bought some great clothes and looked really fine;
he went out each night and
                      tried anything new;
his life was becoming too good to be true!
He forgot about home,
          that was all in the past;
his friends were great fun and his money went fast.
He didn't get work and before very long,
he woke up one morning,
                          and his cash was all gone!

*B*ut feeling too proud to go home to his mum,
he attempted to borrow
                  some cash from a chum,
but those who had loved him with money to spend,
dropped him like a brick when it came to an end,
and soon he was homeless
                    with nothing to eat,
and found himself begging for bread on the street.
He tried to get work but employers just said
they thought he was dirty,
          his clothes hung in shreds.

*T*hen too sick to work hard and too weak to dig,
his only employment
                  was feeding the pigs!

But they gave him no money and they gave him no food,
so he longed to eat pig-swill
        the pigs thought was good! . . .
Then he sat with the pigs in a feverish daze,
and wondered quite how
                he'd got into this maze!

This went on some time until one day he woke,
and shook off his daze
        feeling better and spoke,
'My father has workmen and feeds them all well,
and all I have got is this stinky pig swill!
If I stay here much longer
                        I'll starve half to death.
I'd better go home and with my last breath
I'll beg Dad's forgiveness for all I have done,
as I do not deserve
                to be known as his son!'

So then, straight away, he climbed out of the sty,
and waved the fat piggies
                a sad, fond good-bye,
and set off for home in his rags and his tatters,
all covered in mudpats and foul, pig-swill splatters.

The passers-by stared at him, keeping their distance,

(he smelled very bad and he walked in a trance),
but he didn't care,
      his new life had begun:
he was going back home to his dad and his mum!

*B*ut back at the farm his old mum and dad
were worrying and waiting
          and feeling quite sad.
They'd heard some bad news and longed to give help,
but their wandering son had to come back himself!

*B*ut they always relied
            on their good, older son
who, quiet and steady, just kept working on,
but the father made sure that a man at the gate
kept watch for his young son,
        no matter how late.

*T*hen one day he spotted, away in the haze,
a small, stumbling figure
        come into his gaze.
He was dressed all in rags, he was tired and sore,
and shambled along as he made for the door.
The farmer just looked,
          and then started to run,
so certain that here was his lost, younger son.

*H*e hugged him and kissed him
                    and hugged him some more
and brought him back home through the wide-open door.

*B*ut . . .
          the older son stood and just looked at his dad,
who made such a fuss of his long-missing lad.
'If I'd gone all wrong,'
               he thought wonderingly,
'would father have made such a fuss about me?'
He turned away then, with a shake of his head,
and went back to work
                    in the cold outdoor shed.

'*B*ut Dad,' said the younger son,
                    getting a word in,
'I'm NOT worth your love as I've done so much sin!
I shouldn't be named
          as your son once again;
just make me like one of your own hired men!'

*B*ut Dad wouldn't hear of it, 'Bring the best seat!
Put a ring on his finger
                    and shoes on his feet!
Let's wash off his dirt and bring the best clothes,

then tell all the neighbours,
                       so everyone knows
that my son was lost but he's come back alive:
to me he was dead,
                  but thank God, he's survived!'

The mother and father were in such a state
that they ordered a great feast
                    to celebrate!
They brought in the fatted calf from the field
to make into food for a wonderful meal.
They called in the neighbours,
             and hired a band,
and before very long the dancing began. . . .

But . . .

       someone was missing, and soon they found out
that their good, older son
             was just nowhere about! . . .

So the farmer went searching his barns and his land,
to bring in his son
        for the meal and the band,
but he found that his first-born was hopping mad,
and refused to come in
             with his long-suffering dad!

'I've slaved all these years for you here on the farm!
I've done nothing wrong
                    and I've brought you no harm,
but YOU never gave me a GOAT for a feast,
and now that he's back,
            you've killed the BEST BEAST!'

'That ignorant fool has just WASTED your savings,
on ALL the wrong friends
        and on ALL the worst things,
and now that he's home you expect me to DANCE!
Well! . . . I'll tell you now,
                    THERE ISN'T A CHANCE!'

The farmer was patient and said to him, 'Son,
you KNOW all my wealth
                will be yours when I'm done!
You've always been with me, I love you for that,
but your brother's my son,
        even though he's a brat!
We want those we love to gather around,
for this son was lost and, praise God,
                    he is found!
At least come and greet him, now he has arrived;
we thought he was dead but,
                thank God, he's alive!'

Then Jesus turned back to those who'd complained.
'I'll tell you, he said,
                  and I'll make it quite plain.
We all of us have many bad things to hide,
and even the good son
        was jealous inside.
The angels in heaven will always rejoice
when one lost person responds
                to God's voice,
and turns from his selfish ways and repents:
and those are the people
             to whom I was sent!'

The son who rebelled in this tale Jesus told,
was no shining hero,
        he was not brave or bold.
He was selfish and headstrong and just wanted fun:
it led him to trouble
            and hurt everyone!

No, the true hero was the man's love for his son,
which the son had no right to,
          with all he had done.
The man loved his young son enough to let go,
but he didn't stop watching and waiting,
        and so

when the son came back home,
feeling sorry and sad,
he did NOT tell him off, he was just VERY GLAD!

6.

The Kingdom of Heaven Is like Yeast

He told them still another parable:
'The kingdom of heaven is like yeast that a woman took
and mixed into a large amount of flour until
it worked all through the dough.'
Matthew 13:33

The kingdom of heaven
is like yeast,
like yeast in a good loaf of bread.
The bread made with yeast
is fit for a feast,
but without it
it's heavy as lead.

For bread made from flour that is
very well ground,
from a cereal crop
such as wheat,
should be soft and flexible,
spongy and round,
not solid or
too hard to eat.

The yeast is a miracle mixed
with the flour,
as it secretly spreads
through the dough.
It makes the bread rise and,
in under a hour,
it doubles in size
as it grows.

The yeast, working silently,
rearranges
the texture of bread
as it cooks.
When properly mixed it
completely changes
the way the bread tastes
and looks.

The kingdom of heaven is like yeast
in the bread
as it quietly works in the world
and grows.
The new life from God is the
yeast that spreads,
transforming the people and places
it goes.

7.
The Builder Who Bungled

'Therefore everyone who hears these words of mine,'
said Jesus, 'and puts them into practice
is like a wise man who built his house
on the rock' . . .
Matthew 7:24-29

Wherever he went, whatever the day,
when Jesus was teaching,
he talked in new ways.
He spoke to the people from God's Holy Law,
but he made it sound different
from teachers before.
His new ways of listening and new ways of seeing,
his new ways of doing
and new ways of being,
turned all that they knew right onto its head,
and the people hung onto
each word Jesus said.

But nothing he said changed
the way that they lived,
the things they believed, or the things that they did.
When Jesus saw this he was full of dismay:
he wanted the people
to follow God's way.
So he told them a cool tale to help them to see
they must all take his words very seriously.

There once were two brothers, business men,
who lived in the city, Jerusalem.
They worked very hard,
over many long years,

and both became rich with successful careers.
So they got together and talked
      with their wives,
and planned how the money could change both their lives.
They shared their ideas;
         their plans grew and grew;
they began to dream dreams about what they would do.

But while the men talked the women decided
the best way to use
      the money provided.
The wives said to them, 'We think that it's good
if we move to a better neighbourhood.
It would show your success,
      and it would be cool
for the kids to go a really good school.'

So they got out their map books,
        they talked and they planned
and decided to build on a new plot of land.
Then the men searched the town and the country around
for a place to build,
      till at last they found
a beautiful valley, just outside the city,
where a stream tumbled down and made it look pretty,
and fixed to a post
      with a rusty old nail,
was a battered sign saying, 'Land for sale'!

They looked at each other, this was just the right place,
they loved the fresh air
        and the feeling of space.
Then, exploring the valley from bottom to top,
they each chose a place for their
                        new building plot.

But they didn't know that the place would contain
a secret hidden in the mountains and plain . . .

One brother chose some land way up high,
near the top of the valley,
        where the stream ran by.
It would need a long road to get right up there,
but he loved the big view and the
                wonderful air.
The other one looked lower down, till he found,
where the stream made a river,
                        some good level ground,
and he thought how his children would love it outside,
where the sand was deep and the river ran wide.

Then both brothers went to the landowner's site,
and bargained for land
        at a price they thought right.

They were anxious to start, as they wanted to build
while the summer was hot
        and the weather was still.
So they visited builders and made a wish-list,
but one man was wise
           and one man was foolish,
and nobody knew, despite all the detail,
that one plan would work . . .
               and one plan would fail . . .

They both chose a house with the same grand design.
It was going to be big and spacious and fine,
and soon they had workmen
        clearing the land,
and builders who laid the foundations to plan,
but this was where their troubles began!

For the house on the hill,
        though the workmen were skilled,
had foundations that took a long time to build.
The builders were having
        to dig into rocks,
and make the ground level with big heavy blocks.
But the foundations of the house
          on the riverside land,
went easily into the lovely soft sand,
and before very long
        his walls were up high,

and the roof was in place against the sky.

When he visited his brother up there on the hill,
the wall was as tall as the first window sill.
They'd got way behind,
                              with the work hard and slow,
unlike the house in the valley below.
'Why didn't you build by the river instead,
then your house would be finished,
          like mine?' he said,
and he sauntered back home to choose decorations,
and start the big moving-in preparations.

He couldn't believe that he finally owned
this house in the country,
                              their lovely new home.
Some summer was left for them all to enjoy,
so he took his kids fishing,
                    like he did as a boy.
They swam in the river, where the water ran deep,
they had barbecue suppers on the riverside beach,
and all of this time
          his brother worked still,
to finish the house that was up on the hill.

At last it was done and his brother moved in

in the last days of autumn,
        when winter begins,
but nobody knew that the hills would contain
a dark secret hidden in the cold winter rain! . . .

The two brothers started to settle down
in their cosy new homes away from the town.
They lived in the country,
        and thought it was great,
so they put on a party to celebrate.

The kids all began at a different new school:
the lessons OK,
        and their friends really cool.
Their mums liked the kitchens, all shining and new,
and the big picture windows
        with wonderful views.
Their dads drove to work like they had done before,
it took a bit longer, that was for sure,
but the roads were good
        and the weather was fine,
and the kids were having a wonderful time.

But one day the weather began to change.
It began to get cold,
        and it started to rain,

but the confident brothers thought,
     'We'll be all right:
our roofs and our windows are all watertight!
Our houses are very well built and are strong,'
they explained to their kids,
       'not a thing can go wrong!'

But nobody knew that the weather
     would bring
a catastrophe that would change everything . . .

Then early one morning when they got up for school,
it had rained over night,
      there were lots of deep pools,
and the high up stream was a waterfall
that crashed on the rocks near the garden wall
of the house on the hill,
     and the windows were splashed
as the water rushed by in a headlong dash.

The river, way down on the plain, swirled around,
and the water was rising
       across the flat ground,
across to the house on the riverside plot,
where the children were watching.
        What a shock!

Nobody knew that a thunderstorm
high in the mountains were the river was formed,
was sending a flash-flood
                    to the valley floor,
and swirling the water right up to their door! . . .

The house on the hill was suffering the same,
as the little stream grew so big that it came
and tumbled right up
        to their very front door,
then into the house and across the floor.

All that the people could do was to run.
The children went first, then dad and then mum.
They clambered and climbed
            up the steep mountain side,
till they got to a place that was safe to hide.
When they finally stopped and turned to look round,
the water was flooding
        their house and their ground!

But when they looked out to the house on the plain,
it was almost hidden
           in the thick, heavy rain,
and the house, full of water, was starting to sway,

just as the people were running away.
Then they saw it fall with a
                  massive great SPLASH,
and they heard, on the wind, a terrible CRASH! . . .

The house on the sand, that the brother had built,
was broken in pieces in the mud and the silt! . . .

When they all looked back at the house on the hill,
there was water all round,
                  but it stood firm and still.
It went in the front door, and poured out the back,
but the house on the rock was strong
                  with no cracks!

When the flood went away, after many long days,
and the brothers went back,
          they were both amazed.
They had built their houses with the very same planning,
but the flood destroyed one and left one standing!
When the brothers saw this
                  they both realised
that one had been foolish and one had been wise.

For even a house that is very well planned,

should never be built on slippery sand.
But a house that is firmly
                built on the rock,
is safe and sure through the greatest shock.

'If anyone hears these words that I say,'
Jesus said, 'and listens to them,
        and wants to obey,
he is like the wise man who built on the hill:
the flood came right in but his house stood still.
The foundations were firmly
                fixed to the rock,
so the house was safe through the terrible shock.

'But if anyone hears my words and refuses
to listen to them,
                but instead he chooses
to go his own way, at the end of the day,
then, just like the foolish businessman
who built his house
        on the sinking sand,
he could find that the storms of life will lash
and his life, like the house,
                    could fall with a crash!'

The builder who bungled in Jesus cool tale,
had got it so wrong he was bound to fail!

He built his house to a very good plan,
but he chose to build it
on very wrong land.
He forgot that foundations need to be sure,
to keep the house standing
safe and secure.

'In just the same way,' Jesus went on to say,
'our lives are like houses
we build every day,
and choosing to follow the words of God
will make our foundations as firm as a rock.'

oOo

8.

The Kingdom of Heaven Is like a Seed

Jesus told them a parable: 'The kingdom of heaven is like a mustard seed, which a man took and planted in a field. Though it is the smallest of all seeds, yet when it grows, it is the largest of garden plants and becomes a tree, so that the birds of the air come and perch in its branches . . .'

Matthew 13:31

The kingdom of heaven
is like a seed.
But a seed can seem trivial,
paltry and small.
It's so insignificant,
nobody needs
one little seed, it can easily fall
and lie there unnoticed,
alone on the ground.

But a little black seed that is
lying around,
has deep inside it a living core,
which no-one has seen
and nobody knows,
but somewhere in there
is a hidden law,
which slowly and gradually
makes the seed grow.

Then it quietly puts out
little white roots,
and while you're not looking,
little green shoots,
and one day that seed,

which started so small,
has become a tree
with branches and leaves,
and a trunk that might grow
a hundred feet tall,
with an eco-system set to receive
the birds and the beasties
that help it succeed.

It is hard to believe this can all be achieved
by an insignificant little black seed.

The kingdom of heaven
is just like a seed.
But a seed can seem trivial,
paltry and small.
It might be ignored,
for nobody needs
one little seed, it can easily fall
and lie there unnoticed
in somebody's heart.

But slowly and gently,
perhaps from one part,
a little green shoot
can begin to show,

and while you're not looking,
before you're aware,
a new life from God has
started to grow.

For quietly, gradually
God prepares,
a network of people who
love him alone,
and an unseen kingdom,
entirely his own.

oOo

9.
The Bridesmaids Who Blew it!

Jesus said, 'At that time the kingdom of heaven
will be like ten virgins who took their lamps
and went out to meet the bridegroom.
Five of them were foolish and five were wise . . .'
Matthew 25:1–13

When Jesus was with his disciples one day,
he began to say he was going away.
He would go to his Father,
                    but he loved them all still,
and would come back again,
            when the time was fulfilled.

His friends and disciples were very surprised
to hear what he said,
                    and did not realise
that the teacher they followed was going to die:
they could not believe it,
            nor understand why.
They thought he might just go away for a time,
so asked him, quite simply,
                        to give them a sign:
some thing or event by which they could learn,
that the time was approaching
                for him to return.

But Jesus explained he could not give a sign,
for no-one would know
            of the day or the time.
Even he did not know, yet he was God's Son,
only God himself knew
                of the time he would come.

Then he told them a story to make it quite clear
they had to be ready
                for him to appear.

The Kingdom of Heaven will be like a wedding
where the beautiful bride
                        is ready and waiting
for the bridegroom to take her to live in his home,
but nobody knows when
        the bridegroom will come.

In those Eastern countries, a long time ago,
the weddings were different
                from what we now know.
On the day of the wedding, in the usual trend,
the groom gave a feast for his neighbours and friends.
They came to have fun, and to
        help celebrate
the final, big day of his bachelor state.

They would have a good time, it would be such a lark
that the party would often
                        go on after dark.
Then when they were ready to go for the bride,
a great many people would gather outside.

They'd go with the bridegroom,
             all singing and shouting,
towards the bride's house
             where she would be waiting.

Now here in this wedding that Jesus described,
the father and mother
             of the beautiful bride
allowed her to choose ten bridesmaids-to-be,
and each was as young
             and as pretty as she.
The girls helped her dress and get herself ready;
they tried to amuse her
                     and keep her nerves steady,
but when it got dark, she stayed in her room,
while the bridesmaids went out
             to welcome the groom.

To be chosen as bridesmaid is every girl's wish,
but five girls were wise,
             and five girls were foolish.
The sky was quite dark, it would soon become night,
so they each took their oil lamps
                     to give them some light.
But five girls remembered fresh oil for their lamps,
and five girls forgot . . .
             and left it to chance.

The party was on when they got to the gate,
and no-one could tell them how long they might wait,
but still, it was cool
                    to be waiting outside,
all ready to go with the groom to his bride.

At first they just talked, as they looked all around,
but then they got tired
                    and sat on the ground.
It began to get later, they started to yawn;
it was now very dark, a long time till dawn;
they huddled together,
                              a close little group,
as one . . . by one . . . their eyelids . . . drooped. . . .

The lamp oil got lower,
                              the lights became dimmer,
and soon there was only the faintest glimmer. . . .
The ten weary bridesmaids
                    fell soundly asleep,
worn out by the wait and the watch they must keep.

At midnight they suddenly heard a loud shout,
'Wake up! Get ready!
                    The bridegroom comes out!'

The girls woke up yawning
              and rubbed at their eyes,
then quickly jumped up to watch him arrive.
They picked up their lamps,
                    but had waited so long
the lights were half out and the oil almost gone.

The five wisest bridesmaids then, with one thought,
remembered the bottles of oil
        they had brought.
They filled up their lamps and trimmed the wicks lightly,
and soon their lights were burning brightly.
But five foolish bridesmaids
                    were down in the dumps:
they'd no extra lamp oil to fill up their lamps.
'Oh! Please let us borrow from your oil,'
              they pleaded,
'we simply forgot the spare oil we needed!'

'But none of us has enough lamp oil for two,
our lights will go out
              if we give some to you.
Go down to the shops in the old market square,
they'll sell you some more, we've no oil to spare,
but come again quickly,
        the bridegroom has come:
you mustn't miss out, it's going to be fun!'

The five foolish bridesmaids ran off helter-skelter,
right down to the market
        and the shopkeeper's shelter,
but he was not there, and the shop was pitch black,
and he was in bed in his house at the back.
They went round the back
                and they banged on his door,
and shouted and knocked again, just to make sure,
until, at the window,
        an angry face showed,
and told them to stop all the racket and go!

'We must buy some lamp oil, it's very important!
We want it right now! It's desperate! It's urgent!'
They pleaded and begged him
        until he came down,
his face in the biggest, black, thunder-cloud frown.
They said he was lovely, they said he was nice,
and he sold them the oil
        at exorbitant price!
Then they ran all the way to the bridegroom's front gate,
but when they got there they were
                just . . . too . . . late . . . !

They felt so downhearted, but the next thing they did
was make their way back
        to where the bride lived.

The bridegroom, arriving there
　　　　　　　some time before,
had started the marriage and closed the front door.
The big wedding banquet
　　　　was going full swing,
they heard the loud music, but couldn't get in! . . .

They knocked and they hammered and shouted some more
to make someone hear them
　　　　　　　　and open the door.
The bridegroom himself, came at last to the gate,
so angry that people had turned up so late.
'Oh please sir,' they pleaded,
　　　　　　'please let us inside.
We're sorry we're late, we belong to your bride!'

'But I do not know you!' he said with a frown
and looked the five bridesmaids
　　　　　　first up and then down.
'Her bridesmaids are in here, already, with us,
how dare you create such a horrible fuss!
You're gate-crashers, aren't you?
　　　　　　　　You can't come inside!'
He banged the door shut and went back to his bride!

Those poor, silly bridesmaids, they cried and they cried.

They couldn't have been more upset
        if they tried.
What a horrible shock, what an awful surprise,
but they wouldn't have blown it
            if they had been wise.
If they had been ready they'd be safely inside
with the wonderful groom
                and his beautiful bride!

Then Jesus explained to them, 'When I come back,
it will probably be
        when you least expect.
Be ready and waiting or one day you'll find,
like the poor, foolish bridesmaids,
                    you've been left behind.
The people who lived just before Noah's flood
were eating and drinking
            and falling in love,
and never believed it was going to rain:
there was no place to run to when the flood came.

So no-one will know that the end has begun,
until God decides when
            Jesus will come.
Then two men, while working together, will find
that one will be taken
        and one left behind;
and two women, making some food for a guest,

will find one has gone, and one has been left.

'So,' Jesus said, 'friends, keep watching and pray,
and always be ready,
              you won't know the day,
but one thing is certain, I'll make it quite plain,
at the end of the age,
                    I WILL COME AGAIN!'

This tale of the bridesmaids helped Jesus explain
that he would be coming to earth
          once again,
and when he returned he promised to bring
the Kingdom of Heaven
                and he would be King.
But, in the mean time, they must live for him here
and show out his love
                until he appears.

Then, when he returns in the blink of an eye,
like lightening that flashes
                all over the sky,
the whole world will know he has come from above
to gather together the people he loves.

*H*e'll take them to heaven to live with him there,
to serve him for ever without sorrow or care!

10.

The Kingdom of Heaven Is like a Net

Jesus said, 'The kingdom of heaven is like a net that
was let down into the lake and caught all kinds of fish. When
it was full, the fishermen pulled it up onto the shore. Then
they sat down and collected the good fish in baskets,
and threw the bad away.
This is how it will be at the end of the age.
The angels will come and separate the wicked from the
righteous and throw them into the fiery furnace,
then there will be weeping and gnashing of teeth.'
Matthew 13:47–50

The kingdom of heaven
is just like a net
a fisherman
will cast into the sea,
and the fisherman, naturally,
hopes that he will get
some very tasty fish for his tea.

But a typical net
must be generous and wide,
and the fisherman will usually find
that a whole lot of fish
are collected up inside,
of many different sizes
and kinds.

There are big ones and small ones,
long ones and tall ones
and ugly ones,
you wouldn't want to meet!
There are dark ones and light ones,
grey ones and white ones,
and some that are
very good to eat.

So the fisherman will drag
his net up from the deep
and empty all the contents
on the shore,
and then he can choose
the good ones he will keep
from all the wriggly fishes
on the floor.

The kingdom of heaven
is just like a net
a fisherman will cast out
very neatly,
but God is the fisherman
who casts out the net,
and the world
is the fathoms of the sea.

At the end of the age
when the net will be drawn
and God
will gather all the people in,
he'll sort out the righteous
from the wicked ones,
be warned,
so the kingdom of heaven
can begin.

Then God will send his angels
to choose
the wicked ones
for the furnace fires of hell
and they will never
be with God,
but he invites
the righteous ones
to come
and live in his kingdom home
for ever.